beginners

the perfect guide for new cooks

STEP-BY-STEP

beginners
the perfect guide for new cooks
STEP-BY-STEP

This edition published by Parragon Books Ltd in 2013
LOVE FOOD is an imprint of Parragon Books Ltd

Parragon Books Ltd
Chartist House
15–17 Trim Street
Bath BA1 1HA, UK
www.parragon.com/lovefood

ISBN 978-1-4454-8280-4

Printed in China

Photography by Mike Cooper
Home economy by Lincoln Jefferson
Cover design by Geoff Borin
Internal design by Talking Design
Introduction by Linder Doeser
New recipes by Christine France
Edited by Fiona Biggs

Notes for the Reader
This book uses both metric and imperial measurements. Follow the same units of measurement
throughout; do not mix metric and imperial. All spoon measurements are level: teaspoons are
assumed to be 5 ml, and tablespoons are assumed to be 15 ml. Unless otherwise stated, milk is
assumed to be full fat, eggs and individual vegetables are medium, and pepper is freshly ground
black pepper. Unless otherwise stated, all root vegetables should be washed in plain water and
peeled prior to using.

For best results, use a food thermometer when cooking meat and poultry – check the latest
government guidelines for current advice.

Garnishes, decorations and serving suggestions are all optional and not necessarily included in
the recipe ingredients or method. The times given are an approximate guide only. Preparation
times differ according to the techniques used by different people and the cooking times may
also vary from those given. Optional ingredients, variations or serving suggestions have not
been included in the time calculations.

Recipes using raw or very lightly cooked eggs should be avoided by infants, the elderly,
pregnant women, convalescents and anyone suffering from an illness. Pregnant and
breastfeeding women are advised to avoid eating peanuts and peanut products. Sufferers from
nut allergies should be aware that some of the ready-made ingredients used in the recipes in
this book may contain nuts. Always check the packaging before use.

contents

introduction

This magnificent cookbook with its profusion of superlative and immensely helpful photographs will prove to be an invaluable guide and source of reference for those who are new to cooking and those who still approach it with trepidation. The recipes are clear, easy to follow, beautifully illustrated and utterly delicious, so whether you've never even boiled an egg or you want to build on a little experience you are certain of success every time.

Each recipe starts with a photograph of all its ingredients but this is far more than just a colourful picture – or even less helpful – a montage that is not to scale so that a mushroom looks the same size as an egg. Instead, it serves as an at-a-glance way of checking that you have everything ready before you start cooking. Just comparing the picture with the ingredients arranged on your own worktop or kitchen table will ensure that you haven't missed anything out and when it's time to add the ham, for example, you have already diced it as specified in the ingredients list. If you are uncertain about how coarsely to grate cheese or how thinly to slice aubergines, a glance at the photograph will provide an instant answer.

Each short and easy-to-follow step of the method is explained without any jargon or incomprehensible technical terms. Once again, what you see in the photograph is what you should expect to see in front of you. This is very reassuring and confidence-boosting when you're not quite certain how browned the chops should be before starting the next step. Finally, every recipe ends with a mouth-watering photograph of the finished dish.

Why you need this book
Learning to cook can seem quite daunting and television chefs who chop vegetables at an unfeasible speed while simultaneously making a sauce and a salad and talking to a camera only serve to make the prospect seem even more terrifying. However, once you start, you'll be surprised to discover just how easy

and enjoyable it is to rustle up tasty and nourishing snacks, main course dishes, desserts and sweet treats.

In this book there are 60 fuss-free recipes for all occasions and every taste from pasta to pot roast and from muffins to cheesecake. In no time at all you will have mastered techniques from carving a chicken to icing a cake and have a substantial basic kitchen repertoire at your fingertips. From Get Started through Novice and Intermediate to Advanced, using this book is like having an experienced chef in your kitchen to guide you.

top tips for beginners

> Read all the way through the recipe – ingredients list and method – before you start, so that you know exactly what you will need. Scrabbling about at the back of the storecupboard to find the right spice or rummaging in a drawer for a whisk in the middle of cooking a dish is, at best, irritating and, at worst, liable to result in a burnt offering rather than a delicious meal.

> Collect all your ingredients together and make sure that they are ready to use – visible fat trimmed from meat and vegetables peeled, for example. In addition, do any initial preparation described in the ingredients list, such as grating cheese. Check with the photograph.

> Arrange the plates and bowls of ingredients in the order in which they are to be used. That way, you're unlikely to overlook something. If a number of ingredients, such as flavourings and spices, are to be added at the same time, put them in small piles or in egg cups on the same plate.

> Don't be tempted to skip any stages in the method – they are there for a reason. If the recipe requires milk to be heated before it is added to other ingredients, for example, don't just grab a carton straight from the refrigerator as you may end up with a lumpy sauce.

> Allow plenty of time. If you try to rush, you will be more likely to make a mistake or hurt yourself on a hot dish or with a sharp knife.

> Don't be over ambitious when deciding on a menu. A cold starter or soup prepared in advance ready for reheating and fresh fruit for dessert will give you time to focus on preparing the main course. When you've had some practice and gained confidence you can be more adventurous.

> When adding seasonings, especially hot spices but also salt and pepper, err on the side of caution. Add a little, then taste and, if necessary, add a little more.

> When you have finished with utensils, move them out of your way. A worktop cluttered with sticky spoons, a used chopping board and a gooey mixing bowl is not an efficient space.

> Be careful when cooking with oil and never leave the pan unattended. Do not fill a deep-fryer more than one-third full. If you are unavoidably called away, turn off the heat. More than half of house fires start in the kitchen. Also turn saucepans so that

the handles don't stick out over another ring or the edge of the hob and remember to turn the oven off when you have finished.

time-saving shortcuts

> Ovens and grills take time to heat up, so if you're going to be using either of them, turn them on to preheat when you first go into the kitchen.

> Some ingredients, such as ham, bacon, smoked salmon, anchovy fillets, dried fruit, stoned olives and many fresh herbs, can be snipped into pieces with scissors more quickly and easily than chopping with a knife. Green beans and mangetout can also be trimmed with scissors.

> Tearing salad leaves and delicate herbs such as basil with your fingers is quicker than chopping them.

> To peel garlic, lightly crush a clove with the flat blade of a cook's knife. This makes the skin easy to remove.

> When chopping chocolate, first dip the knife blade into hot water and dry it. Dipping a measuring spoon into hot water, then drying it, makes it easier to measure small quantities of sticky ingredients such as honey and syrup. Speed up cake making by rinsing the bowl with boiling water, then drying before beating together the butter and sugar.

> When boiling root vegetables, such as carrots, make a shallow layer in a large saucepan rather than a deep layer in a smaller pan so that they cook more quickly.

> If the recipe calls for softened butter and you have forgotten to remove it from the refrigerator, microwave it on high for 15–20 seconds.

> The smaller ingredients are, the faster they will cook. Finely dicing and chopping vegetables will speed up the cooking time and if you use a food processor to do this, you will speed up the preparation time.

> You can marinate meat in advance, then freeze it until the day you want to cook it.

> Remember that you don't have to make everything from scratch with fresh ingredients. Take advantage of really useful convenience ingredients, some of which have extra benefits in addition to being time-saving. Canned tomatoes, for example, have far more flavour than imported fresh ones that have to be picked before they ripen. Other useful canned goods include sweetcorn and pulses such as chickpeas. Ready-made pastry dough and prepared vegetables also speed up food preparation without loss of quality.

> Don't throw the ends of loaves of bread away. Tear them up and process to breadcrumbs in a blender

or food processor, then store them in the freezer until required for a recipe. This is economical too. You can also grate lemon and lime rinds after squeezing the fruits for their juice and store in the freezer.

useful equipment

As a general rule, it is worth buying the best-quality kitchen equipment you can afford as it will be more efficient and last longer.

> **Scales:** Some kinds of cooking, such as cake making, really do need accurate measurements and a good set of scales is well worth having. Electronic scales are the most accurate but the batteries must be replaced quite frequently. Spring scales are easy to use and old-fashioned balance scales are accurate but a little fidgety.

> **Measuring jugs:** These are available in a variety of sizes, shapes and materials – a heatproof jug is particularly useful. A tall, thin, translucent jug is easier to use than a short, fat, opaque one.

> **Measuring spoons:** When recipes specify small quantities of ingredients in spoon measurements they mean specific measuring spoons, not ordinary tablespoons and teaspoons. Sets are inexpensive and usually consist of a 1 tablespoon and 1, ½ and ¼ teaspoon. To measure dry ingredients, such as

cornflour, scoop them up in the appropriate spoon, then level off with the blade of a knife.

> **Saucepans:** Start off with three or four different-sized pans with thick flat bases, tight-fitting lids and heatproof handles on both pans and lids. You can add to them as you grow more proficient and assured about the style of cooking that suits you. Avoid sets of pans as they will often include at least one pan that you never need to use and takes up storage space. Non-stick linings are a matter of choice.

> **Frying pan:** A 23–28-cm/9–11-inch heavy-based frying pan with sloping sides has a multitude of uses from frying eggs to searing fish. Non-stick pans mean that you use less fat and are easier to clean, but as sediment doesn't stick to the base of the pan, they cannot be deglazed for making sauces and gravies. A smaller pan is useful for omelettes, pancakes and toasting seeds, nuts and spices.

> **Knives:** Heavy, well-balanced knives are essential in any kitchen. Start with a cook's, utility, paring and vegetable knife and add to them as you go along. A carving knife is also necessary if you plan to cook roasts. Store them in a knife block to prevent the edge of the blades from being chipped and sharpen frequently. Blunt knives are not only inefficient but can also slip easily.

>1 >2 >3

> **Chopping boards:** It is sensible to have several of these and to keep them for separate use with meat and poultry, fish, and vegetables and fruit to avoid cross-contamination. Polythene boards are available in a range of colours, making it easy to know which one should be used for which ingredients, and they can be sterilized. Many people prefer wood which, although it can't be sterilized, is naturally anti-bacterial.

> **Bowls:** You will need various sizes for mixing, whisking and holding measured ingredients. Bowls may be stainless steel, ceramic, copper, melamine, plain glass and heatproof, ovenproof, microwave-proof glass. Some come with a plastic lid, making them useful for storage as well.

> **Sieves:** Wire sieves in various sizes are useful for straining vegetables and sifting dry ingredients. As metal can taint the flavour of acid mixtures, it is also worth having at least one nylon strainer.

> **Spoons, spatulas and ladles:** Wooden spoons are strong, don't bend or break and don't get hot so they are invaluable for many purposes. It is worth buying a selection of them, some with shaped edges. Spatulas, made from wood, rubber or plastic are also multi-purpose and are especially useful if you have non-stick pans. A large slotted spoon helps to drain ingredients as you lift them out of the pan. A ladle with a good size bowl is perfect for transferring liquid or semi-liquid ingredients. Make sure it has a pouring lip or a continuous rolled lip to make it easy to pour without spillage and drips.

> **A hand-held balloon whisk:** These can be used for lots of tasks, such as beating eggs and whisking sauces. A hand-held electric mixer will make such tasks even quicker and easier.

> **Oven-to-tableware:** These dual- or even treble-purpose casseroles and dishes are not necessarily cheap but are good value for money and save time – not so much with cooking, although they can do, but certainly with clearing up afterwards. They may be plain or patterned glass or ceramic and include a vast range of different dishes from casseroles to ramekins. Enamel coated cast-iron casseroles and dishes distribute heat evenly and look smart, but they are heavy, especially when full, and usually not suitable for the dishwasher.

> **Bakeware:** As there is such an extensive range, it is probably sensible to buy cake tins, muffin tins, loaf tins, quiche dishes, and so on, as and when you need them. Heavy gauge tins distribute heat evenly and prevent scorching. They are available with non-stick linings. Baking sheets and trays are used for many purposes in addition to making tarts and pastries, so it is worth buying heavy sheets that won't buckle in the oven or wobble when you lift them out.

get started

easy eggs

serves 4

ingredients

boiled
4 eggs, at room
  temperature

scrambled
8 eggs
4 tbsp single cream or milk
25 g/1 oz butter
salt and pepper

fried
groundnut or sunflower oil
4 very fresh eggs

poached
4 very fresh eggs

>1 Boiled

Place the eggs in a small saucepan and add enough cold water to just cover. Place over a high heat until just boiling.

>2

Reduce the heat to a simmer and cook the eggs for 3 minutes for a soft-boiled egg with a runny yolk.

>1 Scrambled

Beat the eggs in a bowl with a fork. Add the cream, season to taste with salt and pepper and beat again.

>2

Melt the butter in a small non-stick frying pan and stir in the eggs. Stir over a medium heat for 1–2 minutes until almost set, then remove from the heat.

>1 Fried

Heat the oil in a heavy-based frying pan until hot. Carefully break the eggs into the pan and leave to set for 30 seconds.

>2

Cook for a further minute, occasionally tilting the pan and basting the hot oil over the eggs to lightly cook the top surface.

>1 Poached

Bring 3 cm/1¼ inches of water to a very gentle simmer in a deep frying pan. Carefully break in the eggs.

>2

Leave the eggs to cook over a low heat for 3½–4 minutes, until just set with a runny yolk. Remove with a slotted spoon.

Serve immediately.

quick omelette

serves 1

ingredients

tomato & pepper

2 large eggs
1 tsp butter
1 tsp sunflower oil
1 small green pepper,
  deseeded and diced
1 tbsp olive oil
1 tomato, diced
salt and pepper

mushroom & herbs

2 large eggs
1 tbsp chopped chives
1 tbsp chopped parsley
1 tsp butter, plus extra
  for frying
1 tsp sunflower oil
100 g/3½ oz closed-cup
  mushrooms, thinly sliced
salt and pepper

ham & cheese

2 large eggs
1 tsp butter
1 tsp sunflower oil
55 g/2 oz cooked sliced
  ham, chopped
55 g/2 oz Cheddar cheese,
  finely grated
salt and pepper

>1 To start the omelette, break the eggs into a bowl, add salt and pepper to taste and lightly beat with a fork. If you are making the Mushroom & Herbs omelette add the chopped herbs to the eggs.

>2 Heat a small omelette pan until hot and add the butter and oil, swirling to coat evenly. Pour in the egg mixture, tilting to spread, and cook for 5 seconds.

>3 Use a palette knife to draw in the edges of the omelette towards the centre. Continue until most of the liquid is set.

>4 **Tomato & pepper**
Fry the pepper in the olive oil in a separate frying pan for 3–4 minutes until soft. Remove from the heat and sprinkle over the omelette with the tomato and fold over.

**5**

Mushroom & herbs
Fry the mushrooms in the butter in a separate frying pan for 3–4 minutes. Remove from the heat and sprinkle the mushrooms over the omelette and fold over.

6

Ham & cheese
Sprinkle the omelette with the ham and half the cheese. Fold over one side to enclose the filling and sprinkle with the remaining cheese.

Serve immediately.

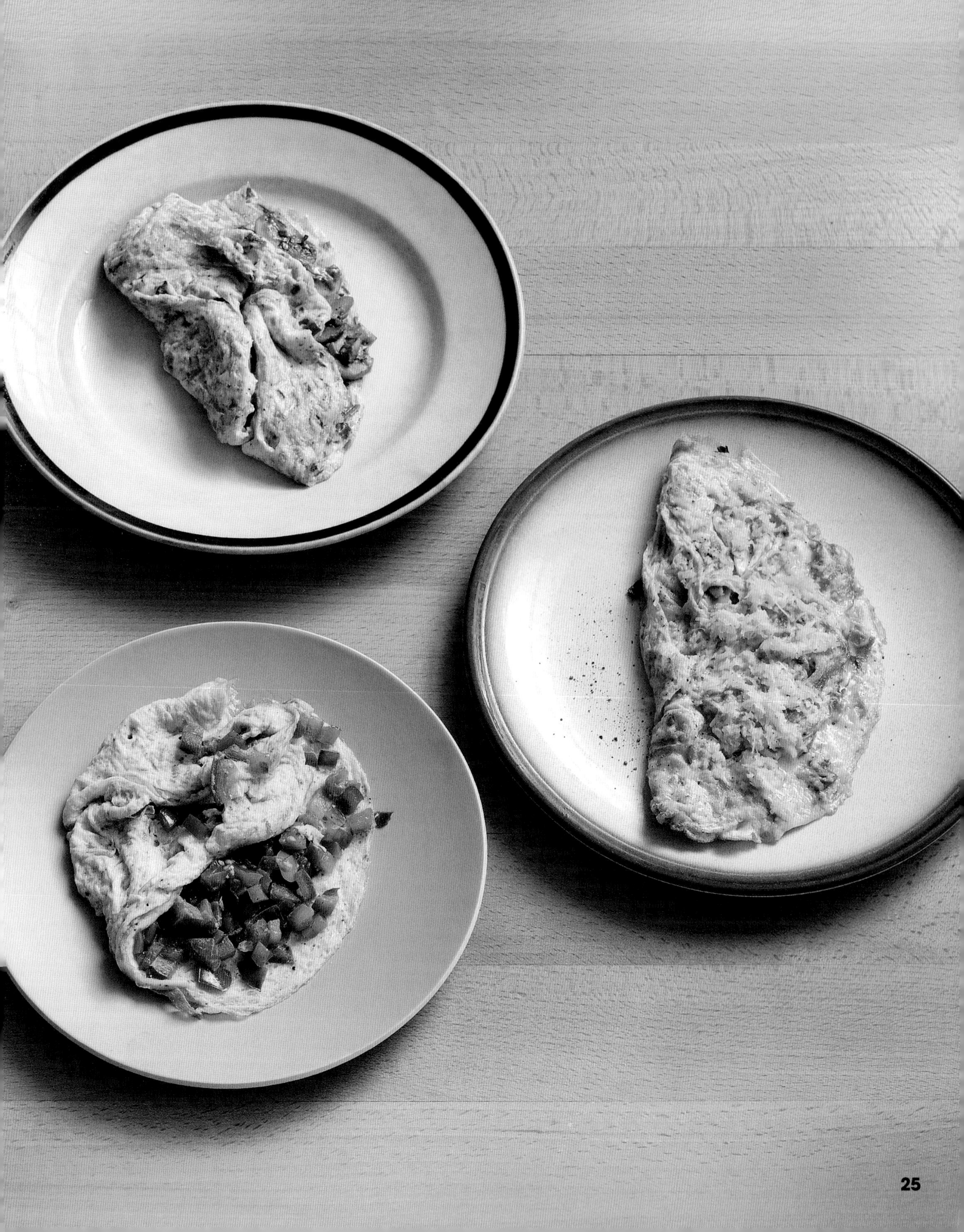

simple fried ham & cheese sandwich

makes 1 sandwich

ingredients

2 slices country-style bread,
  such as white Italian bread,
  thinly sliced

20 g/¾ oz butter, softened

55 g/2 oz Gruyère cheese,
  grated

1 slice cooked ham,
  trimmed to fit the bread,
  if necessary

>**1** Thinly spread each slice of bread on one
side with butter, then put one slice on the
work surface, buttered side down.

>**2** Sprinkle half the cheese over, taking
it to the edge. Add the ham and the
remaining cheese, add the other slice of
bread, buttered side up, and press down.

Cut the sandwich in half diagonally and serve immediately.

>3 Heat a heavy-based frying pan over a medium–high heat. Reduce the heat to medium, add the sandwich and fry on one side for 2–3 minutes, until golden brown.

>4 Flip the sandwich over and fry on the other side for 2–3 minutes, until all the cheese is melted and the bread is golden brown.

perfect steak

serves 4

ingredients

4 sirloin steaks,
  about 225 g/8 oz each

oil, for brushing
salt and pepper

>1 Heat a frying pan or griddle pan over a high heat, until smoking hot. As a general rule, do not cook more than two steaks at a time and keep them spaced well apart. If you add more than two steaks to the pan the temperature will drop too low to successfully fry the steaks.

>2 To prevent the steaks from curling up, cut the fat edge at 1-cm/½-inch intervals with a sharp knife. Lightly brush with a little olive oil and season with salt and pepper. Steaks can safely be eaten rare or blue, but note that cooking times will vary depending on the type and thickness of the steak, and how hot your pan is.

>3 For blue, place the steak in a very hot pan and cook for 1 minute on each side to sear the outside but leave the centre very rare. Leave to stand for 3 minutes before serving. Allowing the meat to rest in a warm place enables the moisture to re-absorb, resulting in a tender and juicy steak.

>4 For rare, place the steak in a very hot pan and cook for 1½ minutes on each side to sear the outside but leave the centre pink. Leave to stand for 3 minutes before serving.

>5 For medium, place the steak in a very hot pan and cook for 2½-3 minutes on each side, so that the outside is cooked and the centre still retains some pinkness. Leave to stand for 3 minutes before serving.

>6 For medium-well done, place the steak in a very hot pan and cook for 3-4½ minutes, so that the steak is cooked through with no pink remaining inside. Leave to stand for 3 minutes before serving.

Serve.

easy roast chicken

serves 6

ingredients

1 chicken, weighing
  2.25 kg/5 lb
55 g/2 oz butter, softened
2 tbsp chopped fresh lemon
  thyme, plus extra sprigs
  to garnish

1 lemon, cut into quarters
125 ml/4 fl oz white wine,
  plus extra if needed
salt and pepper

>1 Preheat the oven to 220°C/425°F/Gas Mark 7. Place the chicken in a roasting tin.

>2 Put the butter in a bowl, then mix in the thyme, and salt and pepper to taste and use to butter the chicken.

>3 Place the lemon inside the cavity. Pour the wine over and roast in the preheated oven for 15 minutes.

>4 Reduce the temperature to 190°C/375°F/Gas Mark 5 and roast, basting frequently, for a further 1¾ hours.

33

>5 To check a whole bird is cooked through, pierce the thickest part of the leg between the drumstick and the thigh with a thin skewer. Any juices should be piping hot and clear with no traces of red or pink. To further check, gently pull the leg away from the body, the leg should 'give' and no traces of pinkness or blood should remain. Transfer to a warmed platter, cover with foil and allow to rest for 10 minutes.

>6 Place the roasting tin on the hob and simmer the pan juices gently over a low heat until they have reduced and are thick and glossy. Season to taste with salt and pepper and reserve.

>7 To carve the chicken, place on a clean chopping board. Using a carving knife and fork, cut between the wings and the side of the breast. Remove the wings and cut slices off the breast.

>8 Cut the legs from the body and cut through the joint to make drumsticks and thigh portions.

Serve with the pan juices, garnished with thyme sprigs.

grilled fish

serves 4

ingredients

olive oil, for brushing
4 white fish steaks or fillets,
  about 175 g/6 oz each

salt and pepper
lemon wedges, to serve

>**1** Preheat the grill to its highest setting with a shelf at a level where the fish will be about 5 cm/½ inch from the heat source. Brush a shallow flameproof dish with oil.

>**2** To remove the skin, place the fish skin-side down and slide a sharp knife between the skin and the flesh, keeping the knife flat.

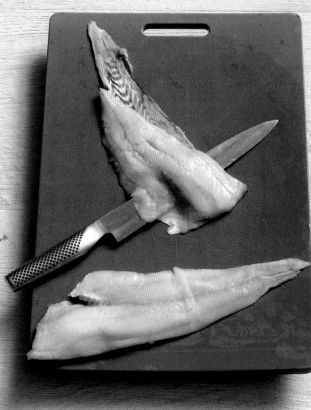

>**3** Brush the fish generously with oil and season with salt and pepper. Lay the fish in the prepared dish.

>**4** Place under the preheated grill and cook for 3–4 minutes until the fish becomes opaque.

>5 Using a fish slice, carefully turn the fillets. Brush with oil and sprinkle with salt and pepper.

>6 Grill the other side for 3–4 minutes, depending on thickness, until the fish is firm and flakes easily with a fork.

Serve immediately with lemon wedges.

vegetable pizza

makes 1 pizza

ingredients

2 tbsp olive oil

1 x 30-cm/12-inch ready-
   made pizza base

3 tbsp tomato purée

1 tbsp chopped fresh thyme

1 onion, finely chopped

1 small green pepper,
   deseeded and thinly sliced

2 tomatoes, sliced

6 black olives, stoned and
   halved

100 g/3½ oz mozzarella
   cheese, torn into pieces

salt and pepper

> **1** Preheat the oven to 220°C/425°F/ Gas Mark 7. Brush a large baking sheet with a little of the oil.

> **2** Place the pizza base on the prepared baking sheet.

> **3** Spread the tomato purée over the pizza base to within 2 cm/¾ inch of the edge.

> **4** Sprinkle with the thyme.

>**5** Arrange the onion, green pepper, tomatoes and olives over the pizza.

>**6** Scatter over the cheese.

>**7** Season to taste with salt and pepper and drizzle with the remaining oil.

>**8** Bake in the preheated oven for 12–15 minutes, until bubbling and golden.

Serve immediately.

quick spaghetti bolognese

serves 4

ingredients

2 tbsp olive oil
1 large onion, chopped
500 g/1 lb 2 oz lean beef
  mince

1 green pepper, deseeded
  and chopped
1 garlic clove, crushed
150 ml/5 fl oz red wine or
  beef stock

400 g/14 oz canned
  chopped plum tomatoes
2 tbsp tomato purée
1 tbsp dried oregano
200 g/7 oz dried spaghetti

salt and pepper
freshly grated Parmesan
  cheese, to serve

>1 Heat the oil in a large saucepan over a high heat.

>2 Add the onion and mince and fry, stirring until lightly browned with no remaining traces of pink.

>3 Stir in the green pepper and garlic.

>4 Add the wine, tomatoes, tomato purée and oregano. Bring to the boil and boil rapidly for 2 minutes.

>5 Reduce the heat, cover and simmer for 20 minutes, stirring occasionally.

>6 Meanwhile, bring a large saucepan of lightly salted water to the boil, add the spaghetti, bring back to the boil and cook for about 8–10 minutes, until tender but still firm to the bite.

>7 Drain the spaghetti in a colander and return to the pan.

>8 Season the sauce to taste with salt and pepper, then stir into the spaghetti.

Serve immediately, with Parmesan cheese.

pasta pesto

serves 4

ingredients
450 g/1 lb dried tagliatelle
salt

pesto
2 garlic cloves
25 g/1 oz pine kernels
115 g/4 oz fresh basil leaves,
  plus extra to garnish
125 ml/4 fl oz olive oil
55 g/2 oz freshly grated
  Parmesan cheese

>1 To make the pesto, put the garlic, pine kernels and a pinch of salt into a food processor and process briefly. Add the basil and process to a paste.

>2 With the motor still running, gradually add the oil. Scrape into a bowl and beat in the Parmesan cheese. Season to taste with salt.

Divide between warmed serving dishes and top with the remaining pesto. Garnish with basil and serve immediately.

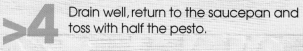

>3 Bring a large, heavy-based saucepan of lightly salted water to the boil. Add the tagliatelle, bring back to the boil and cook for 8–10 minutes, until tender but still firm to the bite.

>4 Drain well, return to the saucepan and toss with half the pesto.

perfect potatoes

serves 4

ingredients

baked
4 large floury potatoes,
  scrubbed
salt

roast
700 g/1 lb 9 oz floury
  potatoes
3 tbsp sunflower oil
salt

mashed
700 g/1 lb 9 oz floury
  potatoes
150 ml/5 fl oz milk
salt and pepper

>1 Baked
Preheat the oven to 200°C/400°F/ Gas Mark 6. Pierce each potato with a fork to allow the steam to escape.

>2
Rub some salt into the skins and bake in the preheated oven for 1 hour 15 minutes, until tender. Cut a crosswise slit in each potato.

>1 Roast
Preheat the oven to 220°C/425°F/ Gas Mark 7. Peel the potatoes and cut into large, even-shaped chunks. Rinse in cold water.

>2
Bring a large saucepan of lightly salted water to the boil. Add the potatoes, bring back to the boil and cook for 10 minutes. Drain, then shake in the pan.

> **3** Heat the oil in a roasting tin and add the potatoes, turning to coat. Roast in the preheated oven for about 45 minutes, turning occasionally, until golden. Serve immediately.

> **1** **Mashed**
Peel the potatoes and cut into even-sized chunks.

> **2** Bring a large saucepan of lightly salted water to the boil, add the potatoes, bring back to the boil and cook for 20 minutes or until tender. Drain well.

> **3** Put the milk in a separate saucepan and heat until almost boiling, then add to the potatoes and mash until smooth using either a fork, hand-held masher or ricer. Season to taste with salt and pepper.

roasted vegetables

serves 4–6

ingredients

3 parsnips, cut into
  5-cm/2-inch chunks

4 baby turnips,
  cut into quarters

3 carrots, cut into
  5-cm/2-inch chunks

450 g/1 lb butternut squash,
  cut into 5-cm/2-inch
  chunks

450 g/1 lb sweet potatoes,
  cut into 5-cm/2-inch
  chunks

2 garlic cloves,
  finely chopped

2 tbsp chopped
  fresh rosemary, plus extra
  to garnish

2 tbsp chopped fresh
  thyme, plus extra to garnish

2 tsp chopped fresh sage,
  plus extra to garnish

3 tbsp olive oil

salt and pepper

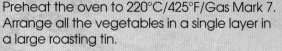

> **>1** Preheat the oven to 220°C/425°F/Gas Mark 7. Arrange all the vegetables in a single layer in a large roasting tin.

> **>2** Scatter over the garlic and the herbs. Pour over the oil and season well with salt and pepper.

Serve with a good handful of fresh herbs scattered on top and a final sprinkling of salt and pepper to taste.

>3 Toss all the ingredients together until they are well mixed and coated with the oil (if you have time you can leave them to marinate to allow the flavours to be absorbed).

>4 Roast the vegetables at the top of the preheated oven for 50–60 minutes until they are cooked and nicely browned. Turn the vegetables over halfway through the cooking time.

easy rice & peas

serves 4

ingredients

2 tbsp olive oil
1 onion, sliced
1 garlic clove, crushed
1 tbsp chopped thyme

400 ml/14 fl oz vegetable
   stock
200 g/7 oz basmati rice
4 tbsp coconut milk

400 g/14 oz canned red
   kidney beans, drained and
   rinsed
salt and pepper

fresh thyme sprigs, to garnish

>**1** Heat the oil in a large saucepan, add the onion and fry over a medium heat, stirring, for about 5 minutes until soft.

>**2** Add the garlic and thyme and stir-fry for 30 seconds.

>**3** Stir the stock into the pan and bring to the boil.

>**4** Stir in the rice, then reduce the heat, cover and simmer for 12–15 minutes, until the rice is just tender.

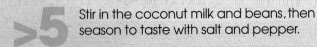

>5 Stir in the coconut milk and beans, then season to taste with salt and pepper.

>6 Cook gently for 2–3 minutes, stirring occasionally, until thoroughly heated.

Serve hot, garnished with thyme.

coleslaw

serves 4

ingredients

350 g/12 oz white cabbage,
  thinly sliced
1 carrot, peeled and grated
4 spring onions, thinly sliced
2 tbsp finely chopped fresh
  parsley

dressing

4 tbsp mayonnaise
2 tbsp soured cream or
  crème fraîche
1 tsp wholegrain mustard
1 tbsp lemon juice
salt and pepper

>1 Combine all the vegetables in a large bowl.

>2 Add the parsley and stir to mix evenly.

Serve.

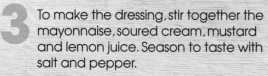3 To make the dressing, stir together the mayonnaise, soured cream, mustard and lemon juice. Season to taste with salt and pepper.

>4 Spoon the dressing into the vegetables. Toss well to mix evenly. Adjust the seasoning to taste.

summer berry tarts

serves 6

ingredients

375 g/13 oz ready-rolled
   sweet shortcrust pastry
250 g/9 oz mascarpone
   cheese

1 tsp vanilla extract
1 tbsp clear honey
400 g/14 oz mixed summer
   berries, such as

strawberries, raspberries,
   redcurrants and
   blueberries
icing sugar, for dusting

1 Preheat the oven to 200°C/400°F/Gas Mark 6. Unroll the pastry onto a worktop and cut into six squares.

>2 Place each pastry square in a 10-cm/ 4-inch loose-based tartlet tin and ease lightly into the tin, without stretching.

>3 Roll a rolling pin over the top of the tins to trim the excess pastry. Press the pastry into the fluted sides with your fingers.

>4 Place the tins on a baking sheet and prick the pastry bases with a fork. Press baking paper into each pastry-lined tin and add baking beans.

>5 Bake in the preheated oven for 10 minutes, remove the paper and beans and bake for 5 minutes. Leave to cool in the tins for 10 minutes.

>6 Carefully remove the tart cases from the tins and leave to cool completely on a wire rack.

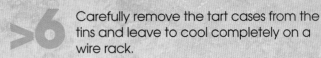

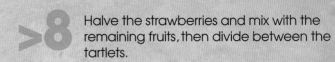

>7 Mix the mascarpone cheese with the vanilla extract and honey, then spoon into the tartlets and spread evenly.

>8 Halve the strawberries and mix with the remaining fruits, then divide between the tartlets.

Dust the tartlets with sifted icing sugar just
before serving.

vanilla-frosted cupcakes

makes 12

ingredients

115 g/4 oz butter, softened
115 g/4 oz caster sugar
2 eggs, lightly beaten

115 g/4 oz self-raising flour
1 tbsp milk
1 tbsp coloured sprinkles

frosting

175 g/6 oz unsalted butter,
  softened
1 tsp vanilla extract
280 g/10 oz icing sugar,
  sifted

>1 Preheat the oven to 180°C/350°F/Gas Mark 4. Put 12 paper baking cases in a bun tray or put 12 double-layer paper cases on a baking sheet.

>2 Put the butter and sugar in a bowl. Beat together until light and fluffy.

>3 Gradually beat in the eggs. Sift in the flour and fold in with the milk.

>4 Spoon the mixture into the paper cases. Bake in the preheated oven for 20 minutes until golden brown and firm to the touch. Transfer to a wire rack to cool.

>5 To make the frosting, put the butter and vanilla extract in a bowl and beat until pale and very soft. Gradually add the icing sugar, whisking well after each addition.

 >6 Spoon the frosting into a large piping bag fitted with a medium star-shaped nozzle and pipe swirls of frosting on the top of each cupcake.

Serve decorated with sprinkles.

perfect pancakes

serves 4

ingredients

150 g/5½ oz plain white flour
1½ tsp baking powder
pinch of salt
2 tbsp caster sugar
250 ml/9 fl oz milk

1 large egg
2 tbsp sunflower oil,
  plus extra for greasing
140 g/5 oz blueberries,
  plus extra to decorate

whipped butter

115 g/4 oz unsalted butter,
  at room temperature
2 tbsp milk
1 tbsp maple syrup,
  plus extra to serve

>**1** To make the whipped butter, place the butter in a bowl and beat with an electric mixer until soft.

>**2** Add the milk and maple syrup and whisk hard until pale and fluffy.

>**3** To make the pancakes, sift the flour, baking powder, salt and sugar into a bowl.

>**4** Add the milk, egg and oil and whisk to a smooth batter.

>5 Stir in the blueberries and leave to stand for 5 minutes.

>6 Lightly grease a griddle pan or frying pan and heat over a medium heat. Spoon tablespoons of batter onto the pan and cook until bubbles appear on the surface.

>7 Turn over with a palette knife and cook the other side until golden brown.

>8 Repeat this process using the remaining batter, while keeping the cooked pancakes warm.

Serve the pancakes in stacks with extra
blueberries, a spoonful of whipped butter and
a drizzle of maple syrup.

novice

quick tomato soup

serves 4

ingredients
2 tbsp olive oil
1 large onion, chopped
400 g/14 oz canned peeled
  plum tomatoes
300 ml/10 fl oz chicken stock
  or vegetable stock
1 tbsp tomato purée
1 tsp hot chilli sauce
handful of fresh basil leaves
salt and pepper

> **1** Heat the oil in a large saucepan over a medium heat, then add the onion and fry for 4–5 minutes, stirring, until soft.

> **2** Add the tomatoes with their can juices, stock, tomato purée, chilli sauce and half the basil leaves.

Serve the soup in warmed serving bowls, garnished with the remaining basil leaves.

> **3** Purée with an electric hand-held blender until smooth, then transfer to the pan.

> **4** Stir the soup over a medium heat until just boiling, then season to taste with salt and pepper.

caesar salad

serves 4

ingredients

125 ml/4 fl oz olive oil
2 garlic cloves
5 slices white bread,
  crusts removed, cut into
  1-cm/½-inch cubes
1 egg

3 Little Gem lettuces
2 tbsp lemon juice
8 canned anchovy fillets,
  drained and roughly
  chopped
salt and pepper

fresh Parmesan cheese
  shavings, to serve

78

>1 Heat 4 tablespoons of the oil in a heavy-based frying pan. Add the garlic and bread and cook, stirring frequently, for 4–5 minutes until the bread is crisp and golden.

>2 Remove the croûtons from the pan with a slotted spoon and drain on kitchen paper.

>3 Meanwhile, bring a small saucepan of water to the boil. Add the egg and cook for 1 minute, then remove from the pan and set aside.

>4 Arrange the lettuce leaves in a bowl. In a separate bowl mix the remaining oil and the lemon juice with salt and pepper to taste.

> **5** Crack the egg into the dressing and whisk to blend. Pour the dressing over the lettuce and toss well.

> **6** Add the chopped anchovies and croutons, discarding the garlic, and toss the salad again.

Sprinkle with Parmesan cheese shavings and serve.

basic beef stew

serves 4

ingredients

1.3 kg/3 ib boneless braising
  steak, cut into 5-cm/2-inch
  pieces
2 tbsp vegetable oil
2 onions, cut into
  2.5-cm/1-inch pieces

3 tbsp plain flour
3 garlic cloves, finely
  chopped
1 litre/1¾ pints beef stock
3 carrots, cut into
  2.5-cm/1-inch lengths

2 celery sticks, cut into
  2.5-cm/1-inch lengths
1 tbsp tomato ketchup
1 bay leaf
¼ tsp dried thyme
¼ tsp dried rosemary

900 g/2 lb Maris Piper
  potatoes, cut into large
  chunks
salt and pepper

>1 Season the steak very generously with salt and pepper. Heat the oil in a large, flameproof casserole over a high heat.

>2 When the oil begins to smoke, add the steak and cook, stirring frequently, for 5–8 minutes, until well browned. Using a slotted spoon, transfer to a bowl.

>3 Reduce the heat to medium, add the onions to the casserole and cook, stirring occasionally, for 5 minutes until translucent.

>4 Stir in the flour and cook, stirring constantly, for 2 minutes. Add the garlic and cook for 1 minute.

>5 Whisk in 225 ml/8 fl oz of the stock and cook, scraping up all the sediment from the base of the casserole.

>6 Stir in the remaining stock and add the carrots, celery, tomato ketchup, bay leaf, thyme, rosemary and 1 teaspoon of salt. Return the steak to the casserole.

>7 Bring back to a gentle simmer, cover and cook over a low heat for 1 hour. Add the potatoes, re-cover the casserole and simmer for a further 30 minutes.

>8 Remove the lid, increase the heat to medium and cook, stirring occasionally, for a further 30 minutes, or until the meat and vegetables are tender. If the stew becomes too thick, add a little more stock or water.

Leave to stand for 15 minutes before serving.

beef burgers

serves 4

ingredients
650 g/1 lb 7 oz fresh
  beef mince
1 red pepper, deseeded
  and finely chopped
1 garlic clove, finely
  chopped
2 small red chillies,
  deseeded and finely
  chopped
1 tbsp chopped fresh basil
½ tsp ground cumin
salt and pepper
fresh basil sprigs, to garnish
burger buns, to serve

> **>1** Preheat the grill to medium–high. Put the beef, red pepper, garlic, chillies, chopped basil and cumin into a bowl.

> **>2** Mix until well combined and season to taste with salt and pepper.

Garnish with basil sprigs and serve immediately in burger buns.

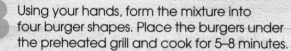

>3 Using your hands, form the mixture into four burger shapes. Place the burgers under the preheated grill and cook for 5–8 minutes.

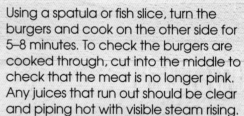

>4 Using a spatula or fish slice, turn the burgers and cook on the other side for 5–8 minutes. To check the burgers are cooked through, cut into the middle to check that the meat is no longer pink. Any juices that run out should be clear and piping hot with visible steam rising.

fried chicken wings

serves 4

ingredients

12 chicken wings
1 egg
4 tbsp milk
70 g/2½ oz plain flour

1 tsp paprika
225 g/8 oz breadcrumbs
55 g/2 oz butter
salt and pepper

>1 Preheat the oven to 220°C/425°F/ Gas Mark 7. Separate each chicken wing into three pieces, discarding the bony tip. Beat the egg with the milk in a shallow dish.

>2 Combine the flour, paprika, and salt and pepper to taste in a shallow dish. Place the breadcrumbs in another dish. Dip the chicken in the egg mixture, drain and roll in the flour.

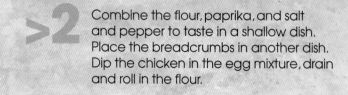

>3 Shake off any excess, then roll the chicken wings in the breadcrumbs, gently pressing them onto the surface and shaking off any excess.

>4 Put the butter in a wide, shallow roasting tin and place in the preheated oven to melt.

>5 Place the chicken in the tin skin side down.

>6 Bake for 10 minutes on each side. To check that the wings are cooked through, cut into the middle to check that there are no remaining traces of pink or red. Any juices that run out should be clear and piping hot with visible steam rising.

Transfer the chicken to a serving
platter and serve.

mozzarella-stuffed chicken breasts

serves 4

ingredients

4 skinless chicken
  breast fillets
4 tsp green pesto
125 g/4½ oz mozzarella
  cheese

4 thin slices Parma ham
250 g/9 oz cherry plum
  tomatoes, halved
75 ml/2½ fl oz dry white
  wine or chicken stock

1 tbsp olive oil
salt and pepper
fresh ciabatta, to serve

>1 Preheat the oven to 220°C/425°F/Gas Mark 7. Place the chicken breasts on a board and cut a deep pocket into each with a sharp knife.

>2 Place a teaspoonful of pesto in each pocket.

 >3 Cut the cheese into four equal pieces and divide between the chicken breasts, tucking into the pockets.

>4 Wrap a slice of ham around each chicken breast to enclose the filling, with the join underneath.

>5 Place the chicken in a shallow ovenproof dish and arrange the tomatoes around it.

>6 Season with salt and pepper, pour over the wine and drizzle with the oil.

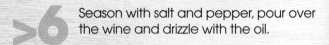

>7 Bake in the preheated oven for 15–20 minutes. To check that the meat is cooked through, cut into the middle to check that there are no remaining traces of pink or red. Any juices that run out should be clear and piping hot with visible steam rising.

>8 Cut the chicken breasts in half diagonally, place on serving plates with the tomatoes and spoon over the juices.

Serve the chicken with chunks of ciabatta.

grilled turkey breast with lemon

serves 4

ingredients

1 lemon
2 tbsp olive oil
1 garlic clove, crushed

4 turkey breast steaks
salt and pepper
salad, to serve

>1 Finely grate the rind from the lemon and squeeze the juice.

>2 Mix together the lemon rind, lemon juice, oil and garlic in a wide, non-metallic dish.

>3 Place the turkey steaks in the lemon mixture, turning to coat evenly. Cover with clingfilm and chill in the refrigerator for 30 minutes. Drain the turkey, discarding the marinade.

>4 Preheat a griddle pan to hot. Season the turkey steaks with salt and pepper to taste, place in the pan and cook for about 4 minutes, until golden.

>5 Using tongs, turn the turkey breasts over and cook for a further 3–4 minutes. To check that the meat is cooked through, cut into the middle to check that there are no remaining traces of pink or red. Any juices that run out should be clear and piping hot with visible steam rising.

>6 Transfer the turkey to a warmed plate, cover with foil and leave to stand for 3–4 minutes before serving.

steamed salmon

serves 4

ingredients
40 g/1½ oz butter, melted
4 salmon fillets, about
  140 g/5 oz each
finely grated rind and juice
  of 1 lemon
1 tbsp snipped chives
1 tbsp chopped parsley
salt and pepper
salad and crusty bread,
  to serve

>1 Preheat the oven to 200°/400°F/Gas Mark 6. Cut four 30-cm/12-inch squares of double thickness foil and brush with the melted butter.

>2 Place a piece of salmon on each square and spoon over the lemon rind and juice. Sprinkle with the chives, parsley, and salt and pepper.

Transfer the salmon and juices to warmed serving plates and serve immediately with salad and crusty bread.

>3 Wrap the foil over loosely and seal firmly with the join on top.

>4 Place the parcels on a baking pan and bake for 20 minutes, or until the fish flakes easily.

macaroni cheese

serves 4

ingredients

250 g/9 oz dried macaroni pasta

600 ml/1 pint milk

½ tsp grated nutmeg

55 g/2 oz butter, plus extra for cooking the pasta

55 g/2 oz plain flour

200 g/7 oz Cheddar cheese, grated

55 g/2 oz freshly grated Parmesan cheese

salt and pepper

> **1** Bring a large saucepan of lightly salted water to the boil. Add the pasta and cook for 8–10 minutes, or until tender but still firm to the bite. Remove from the heat and drain. Add a small knob of butter, return to the saucepan and cover to keep warm.

> **2** Put the milk and nutmeg into a saucepan over a low heat and heat until warm, but do not bring to the boil.

> **3** Melt the butter in a heavy-based saucepan over a low heat, then add the flour and stir to make a roux. Cook gently for 2 minutes.

> **4** Add the milk a little at a time, whisking it into the roux, then cook for about 10–15 minutes to make a loose, custard-style sauce.

Add three quarters of the Cheddar cheese and all the Parmesan cheese and stir through until they have melted in. Season to taste with salt and pepper and remove from the heat.

Preheat the grill to high. Put the macaroni into a shallow heatproof dish, then pour the sauce over.

Scatter the remaining cheese over the top and place the dish under the preheated grill.

Grill until the cheese begins to brown.

Serve immediately.

mushroom stroganoff

serves 4

ingredients

25 g/1 oz butter
1 onion, finely chopped
450 g/1 lb closed-cup
 mushrooms, quartered
1 tsp tomato purée
1 tsp wholegrain mustard
150 ml/5 fl oz crème fraîche
1 tsp paprika, plus extra
 to garnish
salt and pepper
fresh flat-leaf parsley sprigs,
 to garnish

>1 Heat the butter in a large, heavy-based frying pan. Add the onion and cook gently for 5–10 minutes until soft.

>2 Add the mushrooms to the frying pan and stir-fry for a few minutes until they begin to soften.

Garnish with extra paprika and parsley sprigs and serve immediately.

>3 Stir in the tomato purée and mustard, then add the crème fraîche. Cook gently, stirring constantly, for 5 minutes.

>4 Stir in the paprika and season to taste with salt and pepper.

raspberry muffins

makes 12

ingredients

280 g/10 oz plain flour
1 tbsp baking powder
125 g/4½ oz caster sugar
2 eggs

150 ml/5 fl oz milk
100 ml/3½ fl oz sunflower oil
1 tsp vanilla extract

rind and juice of 1 small
  lemon
140 g/5 oz fresh raspberries
icing sugar, for sprinkling

> **1** Preheat the oven to 200°C/400°F/Gas Mark 6. Place 12 muffin cases in a muffin tray.

> **2** Sift the flour, baking powder and sugar into a large mixing bowl.

> **3** Put the eggs, milk, oil, vanilla extract and lemon rind and juice in a separate mixing bowl and whisk together with a fork.

> **4** Stir the wet mixture into the dry ingredients and mix lightly and evenly to make a soft batter.

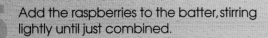

>5 Add the raspberries to the batter, stirring lightly until just combined.

>6 Spoon the batter into the muffin cases. Bake in the preheated oven for about 20 minutes, until firm and golden.

Leave to cool on a wire rack or serve slightly warm, sprinkled with a little icing sugar.

chocolate chip cookies

makes 30

ingredients
175 g/6 oz plain flour
1 tsp baking powder
125 g/4½ oz soft margarine,
  plus extra for greasing
85 g/3 oz light muscovado
  sugar
55 g/2 oz caster sugar
½ tsp vanilla extract
1 egg
125 g/4½ oz plain
  chocolate chips

>**1** Preheat the oven to 190°C/375°F/Gas Mark 5.
Lightly grease two baking trays.

>**2** Place all of the ingredients in a large
mixing bowl and beat until well
combined.

Serve immediately or store in an airtight container.

> 3 Place tablespoonfuls of the mixture on the prepared baking trays, spacing them well apart to allow for spreading during cooking.

> 4 Bake in the preheated oven for 10–12 minutes, or until the cookies are golden brown. Using a palette knife, transfer the cookies to a wire rack to cool completely.

rocky road bars

makes 8 bars

ingredients

175 g/6 oz milk or plain
  chocolate
55 g/2 oz butter
100 g/3½ oz shortcake
  biscuits, broken into pieces

85 g/3 oz white mini
  marshmallows
85 g/3 oz walnuts or
  peanuts
icing sugar, sifted, for dusting

>1 Line an 18-cm/7-inch square cake tin with baking paper.

>2 Break the chocolate into squares and place in a heatproof bowl.

>3 Set the bowl over a saucepan of gently simmering water and heat until the chocolate is melted, taking care that the bowl does not touch the water.

>4 Add the butter and stir until melted and combined. Leave to cool slightly.

>5 Stir the broken biscuits, marshmallows and nuts into the chocolate mixture.

>6 Pour the chocolate mixture into the lined tin, pressing down with the back of a spoon. Chill in the refrigerator for at least 2 hours, or until firm.

>7 Carefully turn out of the tin onto a wooden board.

>8 Dust with icing sugar.

Cut into eight pieces to serve.

strawberry ice cream sundae

serves 4

ingredients

450 g/1 lb strawberries,
 hulled
2 tbsp icing sugar
1 tbsp lemon juice
150 ml/5 fl oz whipping
 cream
500 ml/18 fl oz vanilla
 ice cream
4 tbsp chopped blanched
 almonds, toasted

>1 Place 175 g/6 oz of the strawberries in a bowl with the sugar and lemon juice and purée with an electric hand-held blender until smooth.

>2 Rub the purée through a fine sieve into a bowl, and discard the pips.

Serve immediately.

> **3** Whip the cream until thick enough to hold soft peaks. Slice the remaining strawberries. Layer the strawberries, scoops of ice cream and spoonfuls of cream in four glasses.

> **4** Spoon the sauce over the sundaes and sprinkle with chopped almonds.

intermediate

cream of chicken soup

serves 4

ingredients

3 tbsp butter
4 shallots, chopped
1 leek, sliced
450 g/1 lb skinless chicken
  breasts, chopped

600 ml/1 pint chicken stock
1 tbsp chopped fresh
  parsley
1 tbsp chopped fresh
  thyme, plus extra sprigs
  to garnish

175 ml/6 fl oz double cream
salt and pepper

>1 Melt the butter in a large saucepan over a medium heat. Add the shallots and cook, stirring, for 3 minutes, until slightly softened.

>2 Add the leek and cook for a further 5 minutes, stirring.

>3 Add the chicken, stock and herbs, and season to taste with salt and pepper. Bring to the boil, then reduce the heat and simmer for 25 minutes, until the chicken is tender and cooked through.

Remove from the heat and leave to cool for 10 minutes. Transfer the soup to a food processor or blender and process until smooth (you may need to do this in batches).

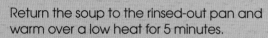

>5 Return the soup to the rinsed-out pan and warm over a low heat for 5 minutes.

>6 Stir in the cream and cook for a further 2 minutes, then remove from the heat and ladle into serving bowls.

Garnish with thyme sprigs and serve immediately.

minestrone soup

serves 4

ingredients
2 tbsp olive oil
2 garlic cloves, chopped
2 red onions, chopped
75 g/2¾ oz Parma ham, sliced
1 red pepper and 1 orange
  pepper, deseeded and
  chopped
400 g/14 oz canned chopped
  tomatoes
1 litre/1¾ pints vegetable stock
1 celery stick, chopped
400 g/14 oz canned borlotti
  beans, drained
100 g/3½ oz green leafy
  cabbage, shredded
75 g/2¾ oz frozen peas
1 tbsp chopped fresh parsley
75 g/2¾ oz dried vermicelli
  pasta
salt and pepper
freshly grated Parmesan
  cheese, to serve

> **1** Heat the oil in a large saucepan. Add the garlic, onions and ham and cook over a medium heat, stirring, for 3 minutes, until slightly softened.

> **2** Add the red pepper and orange pepper and the chopped tomatoes and cook for a further 2 minutes, stirring. Stir in the stock, then add the celery.

Sprinkle with the Parmesan cheese and serve immediately.

>3 Add the beans to the pan with the cabbage, peas and parsley. Season to taste with salt and pepper. Bring to the boil, then reduce the heat and simmer for 30 minutes.

>4 Add the pasta to the pan. Cook for a further 8–10 minutes, or according to the packet instructions. Remove from the heat and ladle into bowls.

meatloaf

serves 6–8

ingredients

25 g/1 oz butter
1 tbsp olive oil, plus extra for brushing
3 garlic cloves, chopped
100 g/3½ oz carrots, very finely diced
55 g/2 oz celery, very finely diced

1 onion, very finely diced
1 red pepper, deseeded and very finely diced
4 large white mushrooms, very finely diced
1 tsp dried thyme
2 tsp finely chopped rosemary

1 tsp Worcestershire sauce
6 tbsp tomato ketchup
½ tsp cayenne pepper
1.1 kg/2 lb 8 oz beef mince, chilled
2 eggs, beaten
55 g/2 oz fresh breadcrumbs

2 tbsp brown sugar
1 tbsp Dijon mustard
salt and pepper

> 1 Melt the butter with the oil and garlic in a large frying pan. Add the vegetables and cook over a medium heat, stirring frequently, for 10 minutes until most of the moisture has evaporated.

> 2 Remove from the heat and stir in the herbs, Worcestershire sauce, 4 tablespoons of tomato ketchup and cayenne pepper. Leave to cool.

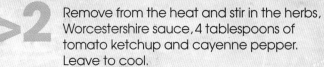

> 3 Preheat the oven to 160°C/325°F/Gas Mark 3. Brush a loaf tin with oil.

> 4 Put the beef into a large bowl and gently break it up with your fingertips. Add the vegetable mixture, eggs and salt and pepper to taste and mix gently with your fingers. Add the breadcrumbs and mix.

129

>5 Transfer the meatloaf mixture to the loaf tin. Smooth the surface and bake in the preheated oven for 30 minutes.

>6 Meanwhile, make a glaze by whisking together the sugar, the remaining 2 tablespoons of tomato ketchup, mustard and a pinch of salt.

>7 Remove the meatloaf from the oven and spread the glaze evenly over the top. Return to the oven and bake for a further 35–45 minutes. To check the meatloaf is cooked through, cut into the middle to check that the meat is no longer pink. Any juices that run out should be clear and piping hot with visible steam rising.

>8 Remove from the oven and leave to rest for at least 15 minutes.

Slice thickly to serve.

meatballs

serves 4

ingredients

1 tbsp olive oil
1 small onion, finely
  chopped
2 garlic cloves, finely
  chopped
2 fresh thyme sprigs, finely
  chopped

650 g/1 lb 7 oz fresh beef
  mince
25 g/1 oz fresh
  breadcrumbs
1 egg, lightly beaten
salt and pepper

sauce

1 onion, cut into wedges
3 red peppers, halved and
  deseeded
400 g/14 oz canned
  chopped tomatoes
1 bay leaf

>1 Heat the oil in a frying pan. Add the onion and garlic and cook over a low heat for 5 minutes, or until soft. Place in a bowl with the thyme, beef mince, breadcrumbs and egg. Season to taste with salt and pepper, mix thoroughly and shape into 20 golf-ball sized balls.

>2 Heat a large frying pan over a low–medium heat. Add the meatballs and cook, stirring gently for 15 minutes. To check that the meat is cooked through, cut into the middle to check that there are no remaining traces of pink.

>3 Meanwhile, to make the sauce, preheat the grill. Cook the onion wedges and red pepper halves under the preheated grill, turning frequently, for 10 minutes, until the pepper skins are blistered and charred.

>4 Put the peppers into a polythene bag, tie the top and leave to cool. Set the onion wedges aside. Peel off the pepper skins and roughly chop the flesh.

>5 Put the pepper flesh into a food processor with the onion wedges and tomatoes. Process to a smooth purée and season to taste with salt and pepper.

>6 Pour into a saucepan with the bay leaf and bring to the boil. Reduce the heat and simmer, stirring occasionally, for 10 minutes. Remove and discard the bay leaf.

Serve the sauce immediately with the meatballs.

pot roast

serves 6

ingredients

4–5 potatoes, cut into
  large chunks
2½ tbsp plain flour
1 rolled brisket joint,
  weighing 1.6 kg/3 lb 8 oz

2 tbsp vegetable oil
2 tbsp butter
1 onion, finely chopped
2 celery sticks, diced
2 carrots, peeled and diced

1 tsp dill seed
1 tsp dried thyme
350 ml/12 fl oz red wine
140–225 ml/5–8 fl oz beef
  stock

salt and pepper
2 tbsp chopped fresh dill,
  to serve

> 1
Bring a large saucepan of lightly salted water to the boil. Add the potatoes, bring back to the boil and cook for 10 minutes. Drain and set aside.

> 2
Preheat the oven to 140°C/275°F/ Gas Mark 1. Mix 2 tablespoons of the flour with 1 teaspoon salt and ¼ teaspoon pepper in a large shallow dish. Dip the meat in the flour to coat.

> 3
Heat the oil in a flameproof casserole, add the meat and brown. Transfer to a plate. Add half the butter to the casserole, then add the onion, celery, carrots, dill seed and thyme and cook for 5 minutes.

> 4
Return the meat and juices to the casserole. Pour in the wine and enough stock to reach one third of the way up the meat and bring to the boil.

137

>5 Cover and cook in the oven for 3 hours, turning the meat every 30 minutes. Add the potatoes and more stock, if necessary, after 2 hours.

>6 When ready, transfer the meat and vegetables to a warmed serving dish. Strain the cooking liquid to remove any solids, then return the liquid to the casserole.

>7 Mix the remaining butter and flour to a paste.

>8 Bring the cooking liquid to the boil. Whisk in small pieces of the flour and butter paste, whisking constantly until the sauce is smooth.

Pour the sauce over the meat and
vegetables. Sprinkle with fresh dill and serve.

pork chops with apple sauce

serves 4

ingredients

4 pork rib chops on the
  bone, each about
  3 cm/1¼ inches thick,
  at room temperature
1½ tbsp sunflower oil
salt and pepper

apple sauce

450 g/1 lb cooking apples,
  peeled, cored and diced
4 tbsp caster sugar
finely grated zest of
  ½ lemon
½ tbsp lemon juice
4 tbsp water
¼ tsp ground cinnamon
knob of butter

> **>1** Preheat the oven to 200°C/400°F/
> Gas Mark 6. To make the apple sauce,
> put the first five ingredients into a heavy-
> based saucepan over a high heat and
> bring to the boil, stirring.

> **>2** Reduce the heat to low, cover and
> simmer for 15–20 minutes, until the
> apples are soft. Add the cinnamon
> and butter and beat until you have the
> desired consistency. Remove from the
> heat, cover and keep warm.

Transfer the chops to warmed plates and spoon over the pan juices. Serve immediately, with the apple sauce.

> 3 Meanwhile, season the chops to taste with salt and pepper. Heat the oil in a large ovenproof frying pan over a medium–high heat. Add the chops and fry for 3 minutes on each side.

> 4 Transfer the pan to the preheated oven and roast the chops for 7–9 minutes. To check that the meat is cooked through, cut into the middle to check that there are no remaining traces of pink or red. Any juices that run out should be clear and piping hot with visible steam rising.

chicken fajitas

serves 4

ingredients

3 tbsp olive oil, plus extra
  for drizzling
3 tbsp maple syrup or clear
  honey
1 tbsp red wine vinegar
2 garlic cloves, crushed
2 tsp dried oregano
1–2 tsp dried chilli flakes
4 skinless, boneless chicken
  breasts
2 red peppers, deseeded
  and cut into 2.5-cm/1-inch
  strips
salt and pepper
warmed flour tortillas and
  shredded lettuce, to serve

>**1** Place the oil, maple syrup, vinegar, garlic, oregano, chilli flakes, and salt and pepper to taste in a large, shallow dish and mix together.

>**2** Slice the chicken across the grain into slices 2.5 cm/1 inch thick. Toss in the marinade to coat. Cover and chill for 2–3 hours, turning occasionally.

Divide the chicken and peppers between the flour tortillas, top with a little shredded lettuce, wrap and serve immediately.

> **3** Drain the chicken. Heat a griddle pan until hot. Add the chicken and cook over a medium–high heat for 3–4 minutes on each side. To check that the meat is cooked through, cut into the middle to check that there are no remaining traces of pink or red. Transfer to a warmed plate.

> **4** Add the peppers, skin side down, to the pan and cook for 2 minutes on each side until cooked through. Transfer to the plate with the chicken.

143

turkey stir-fry

serves 4

ingredients

450 g/1 lb turkey breast,
  skinned and cut into strips
200 g/7 oz basmati rice
1 tbsp vegetable oil
1 broccoli stalk,
  cut into florets

2 heads pak choi, washed
  and separated
1 red pepper, deseeded
  and thinly sliced
50 ml/2 fl oz chicken stock
salt

marinade
1 tbsp soy sauce
1 tbsp honey
2 garlic cloves, crushed

>1 To make the marinade, combine the ingredients in a medium-sized bowl. Add the turkey and toss to coat. Cover with clingfilm and marinate in the refrigerator for 2 hours.

>2 Cook the rice in a saucepan of lightly salted water for 10–12 minutes, until tender. Drain and keep warm.

>3 Meanwhile, preheat a wok over a medium–high heat, add the oil and heat for 1 minute. Add the turkey and stir-fry for 3 minutes. To check that the meat is cooked through, cut into the middle to check that there are no remaining traces of pink or red. Any juices that run out should be clear and piping hot with visible steam rising.

>4 Remove the turkey with a slotted spoon, set aside and keep warm. Add the broccoli, pak choi and red pepper to the wok and stir-fry for 2 minutes.

145

5 Add the stock and continue to stir-fry for 2 minutes, or until the vegetables are tender but still firm to the bite.

6 Return the turkey to the wok and cook briefly to reheat.

tuna pasta bake

serves 4

ingredients

250 g/9 oz dried elbow
  macaroni
375 g/13 oz canned tuna in
  oil, drained and flaked
1 small red onion, grated
2 tbsp chopped fresh
  parsley
200 g/7 oz Cheddar cheese,
  grated
1 large egg, beaten
225 ml/8 fl oz single cream
¼ tsp grated nutmeg
salt and pepper

> **1** Preheat the oven to 220°C/425°F/Gas Mark 7 and place a baking sheet on the middle shelf to heat. Bring a saucepan of lightly salted water to the boil, add the macaroni and cook according to the packet instructions, or until tender but still firm to the bite. Drain.

> **2** Combine the macaroni, tuna, onion, parsley and half the cheese in a shallow, 2-litre/3½-pint ovenproof dish, spreading evenly.

Serve hot.

>3 Beat the egg with the cream, nutmeg, and salt and pepper to taste. Pour over the macaroni mixture and sprinkle with the remaining cheese.

>4 Place the dish on the preheated baking sheet in the oven and bake for about 15 minutes, until golden brown and bubbling.

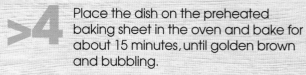

fish cakes

makes 8

ingredients

300 g/10½ oz floury
  potatoes, peeled
300 g/10½ oz cooked
  salmon, flaked
8 tbsp chopped fresh dill,
  plus extra to garnish
6 spring onions, some green
  parts included, finely
  chopped

1 tbsp cornflour, sifted
1 tsp salt
½ tsp pepper
2 eggs, lightly beaten
flour, for dusting
oil, for frying

aïoli

3 large garlic cloves
1 tsp sea salt flakes
2 egg yolks, at room
  temperature
250 ml/9 fl oz extra virgin
  olive oil
2 tbsp lemon juice

>1 Bring a large saucepan of water to the boil, add the potatoes, bring back to the boil and cook for 20 minutes or until tender. Drain well, mash and set aside.

>2 Put the salmon, potato, dill and spring onions into a large bowl and lightly mix with a fork.

>3 Sprinkle with the cornflour, salt and pepper. Stir in the eggs.

>4 With floured hands, form the mixture into 8 patties about 2 cm/¾ inch thick.

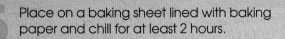

>5 Place on a baking sheet lined with baking paper and chill for at least 2 hours.

>6 To make the aïoli, use a mortar and pestle to crush the garlic and salt to a smooth paste. Transfer to a large bowl. Beat in the egg yolks.

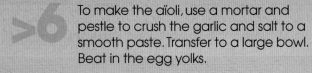

>7 Add the oil, a few drops at a time, whisking constantly, until thick and smooth. Beat in the lemon juice. Cover with clingfilm and set aside.

>8 Heat the oil in a frying pan and cook the cakes over a medium–high heat for 8 minutes, until golden. Turn and cook the other side for 4–5 minutes until golden.

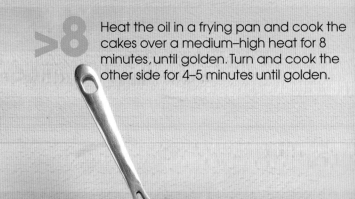

Garnish with dill and serve immediately with the aïoli.

bean burgers

makes 4

ingredients

1 tbsp sunflower oil,
   plus extra for brushing
1 onion, finely chopped
1 garlic clove, finely
   chopped

1 tsp ground coriander
1 tsp ground cumin
115 g/4 oz button
   mushrooms, finely
   chopped

425 g/15 oz canned red
   kidney beans, drained and
   rinsed
2 tbsp chopped fresh
   flat-leaf parsley

plain flour, for dusting
salt and pepper
burger buns and salad
   leaves, to serve

>1 Heat the oil in a heavy-based frying pan over a medium heat. Add the onion and cook, stirring frequently, for 5 minutes, or until soft.

>2 Add the garlic, coriander and cumin and cook, stirring, for a further minute.

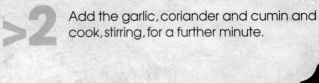

>3 Add the mushrooms and cook, stirring frequently, for 4–5 minutes, until all the liquid has evaporated. Transfer to a bowl.

>4 Put the beans into a bowl and mash with a potato masher. Stir into the mushroom mixture with the parsley and season to taste with salt and pepper.

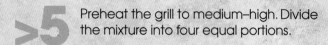

>5 Preheat the grill to medium–high. Divide the mixture into four equal portions.

>6 Lightly dust with flour and shape into flat patties. Brush with oil and cook under the grill for 4–5 minutes on each side.

Serve in the burger buns with the salad leaves.

pasta all' arrabbiata

serves 4

ingredients
150 ml/5 fl oz dry white wine
1 tbsp sun-dried tomato
  purée
2 fresh red chillies
2 garlic cloves, finely
  chopped
4 tbsp chopped fresh
  flat-leaf parsley
400 g/14 oz dried penne
salt and pepper
fresh pecorino cheese
  shavings, to garnish

sugocasa
5 tbsp extra virgin olive oil
450 g/1 lb plum tomatoes,
  chopped

>1 To make the sugocasa, heat the oil in a frying pan over a high heat until almost smoking. Add the tomatoes and cook, stirring frequently, for 2–3 minutes.

>2 Reduce the heat to low and cook for about 20 minutes. Season to taste with salt and pepper. Using a wooden spoon, press through a non-metallic sieve into a saucepan.

Sprinkle with the remaining parsley, garnish with cheese shavings and serve immediately.

>3 Add the wine, tomato purée, whole chillies and garlic to the pan and bring to the boil. Reduce the heat and simmer gently, then remove the chillies. Check and adjust the seasoning, adding the chillies back in for a hotter sauce, then stir in half the parsley.

>4 Meanwhile, bring a large saucepan of lightly salted water to the boil. Add the pasta, bring back to the boil and cook for 8–10 minutes, or until tender but still firm to the bite. Add the sauce to the pasta and toss to coat.

chocolate cake

serves 8

ingredients

150 g/5½ oz plain white flour
25 g/1 oz cocoa powder
175 g/6 oz golden caster
  sugar
1 tbsp baking powder

175 g/6 oz unsalted butter,
  at room temperature, plus
  extra for greasing
3 eggs, beaten
1 tsp vanilla extract
2 tbsp milk

frosting

115 g/4 oz unsalted butter,
  at room temperature
200 g/7 oz icing sugar
2 tbsp cocoa powder
1 tsp vanilla extract

>1 Preheat the oven to 180°C/350°F/Gas Mark 4. Grease and line the base and sides of two 20-cm/8-inch sandwich cake tins.

>2 Sift the flour, cocoa, sugar and baking powder into a large bowl and make a well in the centre.

>3 Beat the butter until soft. Add to the dry ingredients with the eggs, vanilla extract and milk. Beat lightly with a wooden spoon until just smooth.

>4 Spoon the mixture into the prepared tins, smoothing with a palette knife. Bake in the preheated oven for 25–30 minutes, until risen and firm.

161

>5 Leave the cakes to cool in the tins for 2–3 minutes, then turn out onto a wire rack and leave to cool completely.

>6 To make the frosting, beat the butter until smooth and fluffy. Sift the icing sugar with the cocoa and beat into the butter until smooth.

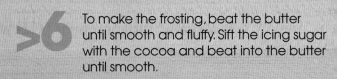

>7 Stir in the vanilla extract with enough hot water to mix to a soft spreading consistency.

>8 When the cakes are cold, sandwich them together with half the frosting, then spread the remainder over the top, swirling with a palette knife.

Cut into slices and serve.

pineapple & coconut ring cake

serves 12

ingredients

432 g/15½ oz canned
  pineapple rings, drained
115 g/4 oz unsalted butter,
  softened, plus extra for
  greasing

175 g/6 oz caster sugar
2 eggs and 1 egg yolk,
  beaten together
225 g/8 oz plain flour
1 tsp baking powder

½ tsp bicarbonate of soda
40 g/1½ oz desiccated
  coconut

frosting

175 g/6 oz cream cheese
175 g/6 oz icing sugar

>**1** Preheat the oven to 180°C/350°F/Gas Mark 4. Grease a 24-cm/9½-inch ring mould.

>**2** Place the pineapple rings in a blender or food processor and process briefly until just crushed.

>**3** Beat together the butter and caster sugar until light and fluffy.

>**4** Gradually beat in the egg until combined.

>5 Sift together the flour, baking powder and bicarbonate of soda over the egg mixture and fold in. Fold in the crushed pineapple and the coconut.

>6 Spoon the mixture into the prepared tin and bake in the preheated oven for 25 minutes until a skewer inserted into the centre comes out clean.

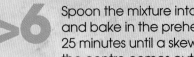

>7 Leave to cool in the tin for 10 minutes before turning out onto a wire rack to cool completely.

>8 To make the frosting, mix together the cream cheese and icing sugar and spread over the cooled cake.

mini apple crumbles

serves 4

ingredients
2 large Bramley apples,
  peeled, cored and
  chopped
3 tbsp maple syrup
juice of ½ lemon
½ tsp ground allspice
55 g/2 oz unsalted butter
100 g/3½ oz porridge oats
40 g/1½ oz light muscovado
  sugar

>1 Preheat the oven to 220°C/425°F/Gas Mark 7.
Place a baking sheet in the oven to heat.
Put the apples into a saucepan and stir in the
maple syrup, lemon juice and allspice.

>2 Bring to the boil over a high heat, then
reduce the heat to medium, cover the
pan and cook for 5 minutes, or until
almost tender.

Serve the crumbles warm.

>3 Meanwhile, melt the butter in a separate saucepan, then remove from the heat and stir in the oats and sugar.

>4 Divide the apples between four 200-ml/7-fl oz ovenproof dishes. Sprinkle over the oat mixture. Place on the baking sheet in the preheated oven and bake for 10 minutes, until lightly browned and bubbling.

169

advanced

lasagne

serves 4

ingredients

2 tbsp olive oil
55 g/2 oz pancetta, chopped
1 onion, chopped
1 garlic clove, finely chopped

225 g/8 oz fresh beef mince
2 celery sticks, chopped
2 carrots, chopped
pinch of sugar
½ tsp dried oregano

400 g/14 oz canned chopped tomatoes
2 tsp Dijon mustard
450 ml/16 fl oz ready-made cheese sauce

225 g/8 oz dried no pre-cook lasagne sheets
115 g/4 oz freshly grated Parmesan cheese, plus extra for sprinkling
salt and pepper

>1 Preheat the oven to 190°C/375°F/Gas Mark 5. Heat the oil in a large, heavy-based saucepan. Add the pancetta and cook over a medium heat, stirring occasionally, for 3 minutes.

>2 Add the onion and garlic and cook, stirring occasionally, for 5 minutes, or until soft.

>3 Add the beef mince and cook, breaking it up with a wooden spoon, until brown all over with no remaining traces of pink. Stir in the celery and carrots and cook for 5 minutes.

>4 Season to taste with salt and pepper. Add the sugar, oregano and tomatoes and their can juices. Bring to the boil, reduce the heat and simmer for 30 minutes.

>5 Meanwhile, stir the mustard into the cheese sauce.

>6 In a large, rectangular ovenproof dish, make alternate layers of meat sauce, lasagne sheets and Parmesan cheese.

>7 Pour the cheese sauce over the layers, covering them completely, and sprinkle with Parmesan cheese.

>8 Bake in the preheated oven for 30 minutes, or until golden brown and bubbling.

Serve immediately.

burritos

serves 4

ingredients

1 tbsp olive oil
1 onion, chopped
1 garlic clove, finely
  chopped
500 g/1 lb 2 oz lean fresh
  beef mince

3 large tomatoes,
  deseeded and chopped
1 red pepper, deseeded
  and chopped
800 g/1 lb 12 oz canned
  mixed beans, drained

125 ml/4 fl oz vegetable
  stock
1 tbsp finely chopped fresh
  parsley
8 wholemeal flour tortillas
125 ml/4 fl oz passata

50 g/1¾ oz Cheddar
  cheese, grated
3 spring onions, sliced
sea salt and pepper
mixed salad leaves, to serve

> **1** Heat the oil in a large, non-stick frying pan, add the onion and garlic and cook until the onion is soft but not brown. Remove from the pan.

> **2** Add the beef mince and cook over a high heat, breaking it up with a wooden spoon, until brown all over with no remaining traces of pink. Drain off any excess oil.

> **3** Return the onion and garlic to the pan, add the tomatoes and red pepper and cook for 8–10 minutes.

> **4** Add the beans, stock and parsley, season to taste with salt and pepper and cook, uncovered, for a further 20–30 minutes until well thickened.

>5 Meanwhile, preheat the oven to 180°C/350°F/Gas Mark 4. Mash the meat mixture to break up the beans, then divide between the tortillas.

>6 Roll up each tortilla and place seam side down in a baking dish.

>7 Pour the passata over the burritos and sprinkle over the cheese. Bake in the preheated oven for 20 minutes.

>8 Remove from the oven and scatter over the spring onions.

Transfer to a serving dish and serve with mixed
salad leaves.

risotto with parma ham

serves 4

ingredients
1 tbsp olive oil
25 g/1 oz butter
1 large onion, finely
  chopped
350 g/12 oz risotto rice
about 15 saffron threads
150 ml/5 fl oz white wine
850 ml/1½ pints simmering
  chicken stock
8 sun-dried tomatoes in
  olive oil, drained and
  cut into strips
100 g/3½ oz frozen peas,
  thawed
50 g/1¾ oz Parma ham,
  shredded
75 g/2¾ oz freshly grated
  Parmesan cheese, plus
  extra to serve
salt and pepper

>1 Heat the oil and butter in a deep saucepan over a medium heat until the butter has melted. Add the onion and cook for 5 minutes until the onion is soft.

>2 Reduce the heat, add the rice and saffron and mix to coat. Cook, stirring constantly, for 2–3 minutes until the grains are translucent. Add the wine and cook, stirring constantly, until reduced.

Spoon onto warmed plates, sprinkle with extra Parmesan cheese, and serve immediately.

>3 Gradually add the hot stock, a ladleful at a time. Stir constantly, adding more liquid as the rice absorbs each addition. Cook for 10 minutes, then stir in the tomatoes.

>4 Cook for a further 8 minutes, then add the peas and ham. Stir and cook for a further 2–3 minutes, or until all the liquid is absorbed and the rice is creamy but still firm to the bite. Remove from the heat, season to taste and stir in the cheese.

individual chicken pies

makes 6

ingredients

1 tbsp olive oil
225 g/8 oz button
 mushrooms, sliced
1 onion, finely chopped
350 g/12 oz carrots, sliced
2 celery sticks, sliced

1 litre/1¾ pints cold chicken
 stock
85 g/3 oz butter
55 g/2 oz plain flour, plus
 extra for dusting

900 g/2 lb skinless, boneless
 chicken breasts, cut into
 2.5-cm/1-inch cubes
115 g/4 oz frozen peas
1 tsp chopped fresh thyme

675 g/1 lb 8 oz ready-made
 shortcrust pastry
1 egg, lightly beaten
salt and pepper

>1 Preheat the oven to 200°C/400°F/Gas Mark 6. Heat the oil in a large saucepan. Add the mushrooms and onion and cook over a medium heat, stirring frequently, for 8 minutes until golden.

>2 Add the carrots, celery and half the stock and bring to the boil. Reduce the heat to low and simmer for 12–15 minutes until the vegetables are almost tender.

>3 Meanwhile, melt the butter in a large saucepan over a medium heat. Whisk in the flour and cook, stirring constantly, for 4 minutes.

>4 Gradually whisk in the remaining stock, then reduce the heat to medium–low and simmer, stirring, until thick. Stir in the vegetable mixture and add the chicken, peas and thyme.

>5 Simmer, stirring constantly, for 5 minutes. Taste and adjust the seasoning, adding salt and pepper if needed. Divide the mixture between six large ramekins.

>6 Roll out the pastry on a floured surface and cut out six rounds, each 2.5 cm/ 1 inch larger than the diameter of the ramekins.

>7 Place the pastry rounds on top of the filling, then crimp the edges. Cut a small cross in the centre of each round.

>8 Put the ramekins on a baking sheet and brush the tops with beaten egg. Bake in the preheated oven for 35–40 minutes, until golden brown and bubbling.

turkey schnitzel with potato wedges

serves 4

ingredients

4 potatoes
2 tbsp olive oil, plus extra for
  shallow frying

1 tbsp dried sage
55 g/2 oz fresh white
  breadcrumbs

40 g/1½ oz finely grated
  Parmesan cheese
4 thinly sliced turkey
  escalopes

1 egg, beaten
salt and pepper
lemon wedges, to serve

>1 Preheat the oven to 220°C/425°F/Gas Mark 7. Cut each potato into eight wedges.

>2 Place the potato wedges in a bowl and add the oil, 1 teaspoon of the sage, and salt and pepper to taste. Toss well to coat evenly.

>3 Arrange the potatoes in a single layer on a baking sheet. Bake in the oven for about 25 minutes, until golden brown and tender.

>4 Meanwhile, mix together the breadcrumbs, cheese, remaining sage, and salt and pepper to taste.

>5 Dip the turkey in the beaten egg and then in the crumb mixture, pressing to coat on both sides.

>6 Heat a shallow depth of oil in a frying pan over a fairly high heat, add the turkey and fry for 4–5 minutes, turning once, until golden brown. To check that the meat is cooked through, cut into the middle to check that there are no remaining traces of pink or red. Any juices that run out should be clear and piping hot with visible steam rising.

Serve the turkey hot with the potato and
lemon wedges.

tuna steaks with olive dressing

serves 4

ingredients
4 tuna steaks, about
  150 g/5½ oz each and
  1 cm/½ inch thick
sea salt and pepper
crusty bread, to serve

dressing
250 ml/9 fl oz
  garlic-flavoured olive oil
200 g/7 oz stoned green
  olives, chopped
4 anchovy fillets in olive oil,
  drained and chopped
4 tbsp fresh orange juice
finely grated rind of 1 large
  orange
½ tsp ground cumin
½ tsp ground coriander
squeeze of lemon juice

> **1** To make the dressing, mix all the ingredients in a non-metallic bowl, add salt and pepper to taste, then cover and set aside for up to 24 hours.

> **2** Heat a large, ridged griddle pan over a very high heat. Brush one side of each tuna steak with dressing, then place in the pan and cook for 2 minutes.

Serve immediately with crusty bread.

>3 Brush the other side with dressing, then turn, season to taste with salt and pepper and cook for a further 30 seconds for rare or up to 2 minutes for well done.

>4 Transfer to plates and spoon a little of the dressing over each steak.

paella

serves 6–8

ingredients

6 tbsp olive oil
6–8 boned chicken thighs
140 g/5 oz Spanish chorizo
 sausage, sliced
2 large onions, chopped
4 large garlic cloves,
 crushed

1 tsp mild or hot Spanish
 paprika
350 g/12 oz paella rice,
 rinsed and drained
100 g/3½ oz French beans,
 chopped
125 g/4½ oz frozen peas

1.3 litres/2¼ pints fish stock
½ tsp saffron threads,
 soaked in 2 tbsp hot water
16 live mussels, soaked in
 salted water for 10 minutes
16 raw prawns, peeled and
 deveined

2 red peppers, halved and
 deseeded, then grilled,
 peeled and sliced
salt and pepper
freshly chopped parsley,
 to garnish

>1 Heat 3 tablespoons of the oil in a 30-cm/ 12-inch paella pan or casserole. Cook the chicken over a medium–high heat, turning frequently for 5 minutes, until golden and crisp. To check that the meat is cooked through, cut into the middle to check that there are no remaining traces of pink or red. Any juices that run out should be clear and piping hot with visible steam rising.

>2 Using a slotted spoon, transfer to a bowl.

>3 Add the chorizo to the pan and cook, stirring, for 1 minute, or until beginning to crisp, then add to the chicken.

>4 Heat the remaining oil in the pan, add the onions and cook, stirring, for 2 minutes.

193

5 Add the garlic and paprika and cook for a further 3 minutes, or until the onions are soft but not brown.

6 Add the rice, beans and peas and stir until coated in oil. Return the chicken and chorizo and any accumulated juices to the pan.

7 Stir in the stock, saffron and its soaking liquid, and salt and pepper to taste and bring to the boil, stirring. Reduce the heat to low and simmer, uncovered, for 15 minutes.

8 Discard any mussels with broken shells and any that refuse to close when tapped. Arrange the mussels, prawns and peppers on top. Cover and simmer for 5 minutes until the prawns turn pink and the mussels open. Discard any mussels that remain closed. Ensure the chicken is cooked throug

Garnish with the parsley and serve
immediately.

prawn noodle bowl

serves 4

ingredients

200 g/7 oz rice noodles
2 tbsp groundnut oil
85 g/3 oz unsalted peanuts
1 bunch of spring onions,
  diagonally sliced

2 celery sticks, trimmed and
  diagonally sliced
1 red pepper, deseeded
  and thinly sliced
1 fresh bird's eye chilli, sliced

1 lemon grass stalk, crushed
400 ml/14 fl oz fish stock or
  chicken stock
225 ml/8 fl oz coconut milk
2 tsp Thai fish sauce

350 g/12 oz cooked peeled
  tiger prawns
salt and pepper
3 tbsp chopped fresh
  coriander, to garnish

> **1** Put the noodles into a bowl, cover with boiling water, and leave to stand for 4 minutes until tender. Drain.

> **2** Heat a wok over a medium–high heat, then add the oil. Add the peanuts and stir-fry for 1–2 minutes until golden. Lift out with a slotted spoon.

> **3** Add the spring onions, celery and red pepper and stir-fry over a high heat for 1–2 minutes.

> **4** Add the chilli, lemon grass, stock, coconut milk and fish sauce and bring to the boil.

> **5** Stir in the prawns, then return to the boil, stirring.

> **6** Season to taste with salt and pepper, then add the noodles.

Serve in warmed bowls, sprinkled with coriander and black pepper and the toasted peanuts.

nut roast

serves 4

ingredients

2 tbsp olive oil, plus extra
  for brushing
1 large onion, finely
  chopped
100 g/3½ oz ground
  almonds
100 g/3½ oz cashew nuts,
  finely chopped
55 g/2 oz fresh wholemeal
  breadcrumbs
100 ml/3½ fl oz vegetable
  stock
finely grated rind and juice
  of 1 small lemon
1 tbsp finely chopped
  rosemary leaves
salt and pepper
fresh rosemary sprigs and
  lemon slices, to garnish

>1 Preheat the oven to 200°C/400°F/Gas Mark 6.
Brush a 700-ml/1¼-pint loaf tin with oil and line
with baking paper.

>2 Heat the oil in a large saucepan, add
the onion and fry over a medium heat,
stirring, for 3–4 minutes until soft.

Turn out and serve hot, garnished with rosemary sprigs, lemon slices and extra black pepper.

> **>3** Stir in the almonds, cashew nuts, breadcrumbs, stock, lemon rind and juice and rosemary. Season to taste with salt and pepper and stir well to mix.

> **>4** Press the mixture into the prepared tin, brush with oil and bake in the preheated oven for 30–35 minutes, until golden brown and firm.

aubergine gratin

serves 2

ingredients

4 tbsp olive oil
2 onions, finely chopped
2 garlic cloves, very finely
   chopped
2 aubergines, thickly sliced

3 tbsp chopped fresh
   flat-leaf parsley, plus extra
   sprigs to garnish
½ tsp dried thyme

400 g/14 oz canned
   chopped tomatoes
175 g/6 oz mozzarella
   cheese, coarsely grated

6 tbsp freshly grated
   Parmesan cheese
salt and pepper

>1
Heat the oil in a flameproof casserole over a medium heat. Add the onions and cook for 5 minutes, or until soft.

>2
Add the garlic and cook for a few seconds, or until just beginning to colour. Using a slotted spoon, transfer the onion mixture to a plate.

>3
Add the aubergine slices to the casserole in batches and cook until lightly browned. Transfer to another plate.

>4
Preheat the oven to 200°C/400°F/ Gas Mark 6. Arrange a layer of aubergine slices in the base of the casserole or a shallow ovenproof dish.

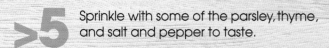

>5 Sprinkle with some of the parsley, thyme, and salt and pepper to taste.

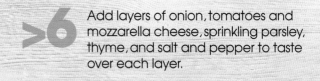

>6 Add layers of onion, tomatoes and mozzarella cheese, sprinkling parsley, thyme, and salt and pepper to taste over each layer.

>7 Continue layering, finishing with a layer of aubergine slices.

>8 Sprinkle with the Parmesan cheese and bake, uncovered, in the preheated oven for 20–30 minutes, or until the top is golden and the aubergines are tender.

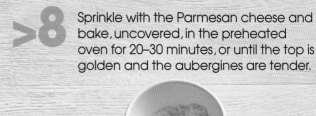

Serve hot, garnished with parsley sprigs.

chilli bean stew

serves 4–6

ingredients

2 tbsp olive oil
1 onion, chopped
2–4 garlic cloves, chopped
2 fresh red chillies, deseeded
  and sliced
225 g/8 oz canned kidney
beans, drained and rinsed
225 g/8 oz canned cannellini
  beans, drained and rinsed
225 g/8 oz canned chickpeas,
  drained and rinsed
1 tbsp tomato purée
700–850 ml/1¼–1½ pints
vegetable stock
1 red pepper, deseeded and
  chopped
4 tomatoes, chopped
175 g/6 oz shelled fresh broad
  beans
1 tbsp chopped fresh coriander,
  plus extra to garnish
soured cream, to serve
paprika, to garnish

> **1** Heat the oil in a large, heavy-based saucepan with a tight-fitting lid. Add the onion, garlic and chillies and cook, stirring frequently, for 5 minutes until soft.

> **2** Add the kidney beans, cannellini beans and chickpeas. Blend the tomato purée with a little of the stock and pour over the bean mixture, then add the remaining stock.

206

Garnish with the remaining chopped coriander and a pinch of paprika and serve topped with spoonfuls of soured cream.

>3 Bring to the boil, then reduce the heat and simmer for 10–15 minutes. Add the red pepper, tomatoes and broad beans.

>4 Simmer for a further 15–20 minutes or until all the vegetables are tender. Stir in most of the chopped coriander.

mixed seed bread

makes 1 loaf

ingredients

375 g/13 oz strong white
  flour, plus extra for dusting
125 g/4½ oz rye flour
1½ tbsp skimmed milk
  powder
1½ tsp salt

1 tbsp soft light brown sugar
1 tsp easy-blend dried yeast
1½ tbsp sunflower oil, plus
  extra for greasing and
  brushing
2 tsp lemon juice

300 ml/10 fl oz lukewarm
  water
1 tsp caraway seeds
½ tsp poppy seeds
½ tsp sesame seeds

topping

1 egg beaten with
  1 tbsp water
1 tbsp sunflower seeds

> 1 Place the white flour, rye flour, milk powder, salt, sugar and yeast in a large bowl. Pour in the oil and add the lemon juice and water.

> 2 Stir in the seeds and mix well to make a smooth dough. Turn out onto a lightly floured surface and knead well for about 10 minutes until smooth.

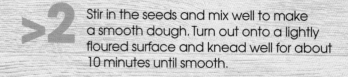

> 3 Brush a bowl with oil. Shape the dough into a ball, place in the bowl and cover with a damp tea towel.

> 4 Leave to rise in a warm place for 1 hour, until the dough has doubled in volume. Oil a 900-g/2-lb loaf tin.

>5 Turn out the dough onto a lightly floured surface and knead for 1 minute until smooth. Shape into a loaf the length of the tin and three times the width.

>6 Fold the dough in three lengthways and place in the tin with the join underneath. Cover and leave in a warm place for 30 minutes until it has risen above the tin.

>7 Preheat the oven to 220°C/425°F/Gas Mark 7. Brush the egg and water glaze over the loaf, then gently press the sunflower seeds all over the top.

>8 Bake in the preheated oven for 30 minutes, or until golden brown and hollow on the base when tapped.

Transfer to a wire rack to cool.

strawberry cheesecake

serves 8

ingredients

base

55 g/2 oz unsalted butter
200 g/7 oz digestive biscuits,
   crushed
85 g/3 oz chopped walnuts

filling

450 g/1 lb mascarpone
   cheese
2 eggs, beaten
3 tbsp caster sugar

250 g/9 oz white chocolate,
   broken into pieces
300 g/10½ oz strawberries,
   hulled and quartered

topping

175 g/6 oz mascarpone
   cheese
50 g/1¾ oz white chocolate
   shavings
4 strawberries, halved

> **1** Preheat the oven to 150°C/300°F/Gas Mark 2. Melt the butter in a saucepan over a low heat and stir in the crushed biscuits and walnuts.

> **2** Spoon into a 23-cm/9-inch springform cake tin and press evenly over the base with the back of a spoon. Set aside.

> **3** To make the filling, beat the mascarpone cheese in a bowl until smooth, then beat in the eggs and sugar.

> **4** Melt the white chocolate in a heatproof bowl set over a saucepan of gently simmering water, stirring until smooth. Remove from the heat and leave to cool slightly, then stir into the cheese mixture. Stir in the strawberries.

>5 Spoon the mixture into the cake tin, spread evenly and smooth the surface. Bake in the preheated oven for 1 hour, or until just firm.

>6 Turn off the oven and leave the cheesecake inside with the door slightly ajar until completely cold. Transfer to a serving plate.

Spread the mascarpone cheese on top, decorate with the chocolate shavings and the strawberry halves and serve.

lemon meringue pie

serves 6–8

ingredients

pastry

150 g/5½ oz plain flour,
  plus extra for dusting
85 g/3 oz butter, cut into
  small pieces, plus extra for
  greasing

35 g/1¼ oz icing sugar, sifted
finely grated rind of
  ½ lemon
½ egg yolk, beaten
1½ tbsp milk

filling

3 tbsp cornflour
300 ml/10 fl oz water
juice and grated rind of
  2 lemons
175 g/6 oz caster sugar
2 eggs, separated

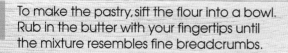

1 To make the pastry, sift the flour into a bowl. Rub in the butter with your fingertips until the mixture resembles fine breadcrumbs.

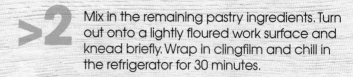

2 Mix in the remaining pastry ingredients. Turn out onto a lightly floured work surface and knead briefly. Wrap in clingfilm and chill in the refrigerator for 30 minutes.

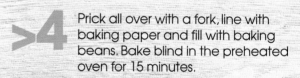

3 Preheat the oven to 180°C/350°F/Gas Mark 4. Grease a 20-cm/8-inch round tart tin. Roll out the pastry to a thickness of 5 mm/¼ inch, then use to line the tin.

4 Prick all over with a fork, line with baking paper and fill with baking beans. Bake blind in the preheated oven for 15 minutes.

> **5** Remove the pastry case from the oven and take out the paper and beans. Reduce the oven temperature to 150°C/300°F/Gas Mark 2.

> **6** To make the filling, mix the cornflour with a little of the water to form a paste. Put the remaining water in a saucepan. Stir in the lemon juice, lemon rind and cornflour paste.

> **7** Bring to the boil, stirring. Cook for 2 minutes. Leave to cool slightly. Stir in 5 tablespoons of the caster sugar and the egg yolks. Pour into the pastry case.

> **8** Whisk the egg whites until stiff. Gradually whisk in the remaining caster sugar and spread over the pie. Return to the oven and bake for a further 40 minutes.

Remove from the oven, leave to
cool and serve.

chocolate mousse

serves 4–6

ingredients

225 g/8 oz plain chocolate,
  chopped
2 tbsp brandy, Grand
  Marnier or Cointreau
4 tbsp water
30 g/1 oz unsalted butter,
  diced
3 large eggs, separated
¼ tsp cream of tartar
55 g/2 oz sugar
125 ml/4 fl oz double cream

> **1** Put the chocolate, brandy and water in a heatproof bowl set over a small saucepan over a low heat and stir until smooth. Remove from the heat. Beat in the butter and then the egg yolks, one at a time, until blended. Cool slightly.

> **2** Meanwhile, beat the egg whites in a clean bowl until holding soft peaks. Sprinkle over the cream of tartar, then gradually add the sugar, beating until holding stiff peaks.

Spoon the mousse into bowls. Cover with clingfilm and chill for at least 3 hours before serving.

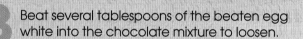

>3 Beat several tablespoons of the beaten egg white into the chocolate mixture to loosen.

>4 Whip the cream until holding soft peaks. Spoon the cream over the chocolate mixture, then add the remaining egg whites mixture. Use a spatula to fold the chocolate into the cream and egg whites mixture.

Index